Being Hur

Waking Up
A New Human Rite of Passage

By Fran Boudreaux

Copyright © 2024 Fran Boudreaux/Being Human, Inc.
Illustrations and cover art by Jennifer Wessmiller
Edited by Valerie Banks Amster
All rights reserved. No parts of this book may be reproduced or used in any manner without the prior written permission of the copyright owner, except for the use of brief quotations in a book review.
Published by Being Human, Inc.
www.beinghumaninc.com
PO Box 273
Warrenton, VA 20188
United States of America
First Edition: February 1, 2025
ISBN 9798302015396

Dedication

This book is written with profound love and respect for all of those awakened and awakening souls out there, seeking truth and navigating their way in a newfound reality. I want you to know that:
- You are not alone.
- You are here on purpose.
- You are an important part of our human collective awakening story and everything you do will make, and is making, a profound difference.
- You are amazing and deeply admired.

This book is dedicated to my amazing family. John, Shane, Pierce, Cody, and Nate, thank you for supporting me through my awakening journey. Thank you for giving me the space, love, and respect to grow and change. Thank you for being my rocks. I love and appreciate all of you more than you know.

Table of Contents

Dedication 1

Introduction 4

Part I 6

Chapter 1 6

Chapter 2 13

Chapter 3 15

Chapter 4 20

Chapter 5 27

Chapter 6 39

Part II 48

Chapter 7 48

Chapter 8 57

Part III 67

Chapter 9 67

Chapter 10 77

Endnotes 80

Introduction

> "The search for reality is the most dangerous of all undertakings for it will destroy the world in which you live."
> –Nisargadatta Maharaj

Reality, defined as "the quality or state of being real" (Merriam-Webster.com), is a concept that is often referenced but rarely understood. Throughout my life, I have heard comments like "Get real!" or "That can't possibly be real," but what is real, anyways? We use the concept of reality to define a way of thinking and perceiving life that we have collectively agreed upon as fact, truth, and static. But is it? Is reality truly real, or is it fluid based on human perception?

When I started my human awakening journey in 2020, I quickly learned that the latter is true. Reality is based on human perception – an awareness that is malleable and easily molded under the right circumstances. Is the reality that we grew up in real, or it is something that we were taught –something that went unquestioned until we started to wake up?

Humanity's process of waking up, both individually and collectively, has been brought about by the expansion of human consciousness. Though this is happening to each of us at different rates and is currently the road less traveled, soon more and more people will begin to awaken, and will be looking for answers and support when they do.

The human awakening journey – what I call a new Human Rite of Passage – is a reality-shattering process that will shake the foundation of your current "known knowns" about your life and about reality. At the same time, you will uncover both disturbing and empowering "unknown unknowns" about our world and about what it actually means to be human.

Waking up can be difficult to navigate, but you are not alone. My intention for this book is to provide a roadmap that can help you as you start to wake up and begin to process all you are learning, and as you seek guidance on how to powerfully move forward.

This book is broken into three parts. Part I defines the concept of "waking up" and describes some prominent attributes associated with the experience. This part also takes you through the four distinct stages associated with the human awakening journey – this new Human Rite of Passage – and puts you on a path to discover your power and begin the process of redefining yourself and your purpose with conscious and proactive intent.

Part II details my journey of awakening and walks you through my thought process and approach when it was time for me to redefine my purpose and create a new game plan for my life after I woke up. This part of the book provides context to be used as a framework to assist you as you also begin to redefine yourself and create a powerful new vision and purpose for your life.

Part III offers some tips to help guide you as you move forward and want to birth your new game and newly defined purpose and vision into manifested reality. Part III also powerfully reminds you of your key role in our collective human awakening story. It is a powerful "call to action" and a plea for all awakened souls to listen to their intuitive guidance system and heed its call. All of us hold an important piece of the collective human awakening puzzle. **The time to act is now. You are important. We need you!** I love you.

Part I

Chapter 1
You Are Not Crazy. You are Waking Up.
Wake Up: *To cease sleeping; to become awake. To become aware or to make aware.*
—Merriam-Webster.com

The first order of business is to define what "waking up" actually means. The best way I can describe it is to start at the beginning of a typical human life. When we are born, we are born into a specific worldview or perception of reality, based on the environment and external circumstances associated with our birth. Our worldview and discernment of reality are typically shaped by our parents or adult caregivers, and then cemented throughout our lives by public institutions such as school and religious organizations, as well as through the content that we consume through mass media including news, social media, television, and movies. It's interesting to think about: Even though we are all having a collective human experience, reality is really more individual, based on life circumstances and external situations.

Reality is an internal experience as well. Whether people realize it or not, we all develop what I like to refer to as a "game of life" that we play, based on our worldview and view of life. Our game of life starts with what we have consciously, or often unconsciously, defined as a successful life, and includes corresponding strategies to achieve this desired goal. This individual game of life sets a course for our lifetime and informs our personality, motivations, and strategies for how we live our lives.

Whether or not they are aware of their individual games of life, most people do not regularly question their worldviews and versions of reality unless or until something tragic happens. Often a traumatic event, such as an illness or a loss of a loved one, results in questioning life and searching for a deeper meaning to existence. Most of the time, however, we keep our heads down doing life, and are usually so busy and distracted getting somewhere that we don't have the time nor the energy to really delve into the more esoteric and philosophical topics of life or our reality. It is rare that people question such important things as "Who am I?" or "Where am I?" or even "Why am I?" People are typically just too busy for these types of questions *to even occur* to them to ask or ponder. They are more concerned about getting through school, paying bills, raising children, and trying to find some fun in our very busy and hurried lives. This is just normal life until you start to wake up.

Waking Up Described

Many religions and philosophies teach that life, and our world, are merely illusions, and that human beings live a somewhat dreamlike existence. Some of the great spiritual traditions of India believe in a concept called Maya, which teaches that the world is an illusion or "unreality." (vedanet.com 2018) Some Native American cultures believe in a concept called Wetiko, which is sometimes referred to as a "sickness of the spirit" or "a contagious psycho-spiritual disease of the soul that is currently being acted out en masse on the world stage via an insidious collective psychosis of titanic proportions." (Innertraditions.com 2022) These beliefs are based on the concept that human beings are sleepwalking through life in a type of unconscious state in a world that may or may not even be real. Could waking up actually be an awakening from some type of a hypnotic state? Could it be the end of a lifelong dream? Could it be an awakening to the fact that the world and life are merely an illusion?

Waking up, in a nutshell, is an expansion of human consciousness. It is analogous to that of the zoom on a camera lens. The zoom feature of a camera lens allows you to zoom in and zoom out to obtain the image you want to capture. When you zoom in on a subject, you are able to take a closer and more detailed picture by focusing just on the subject and excluding any surrounding area. On the contrary, when you zoom out, you take a more panoramic view, which captures the subject but from a larger, more expanded perspective.

In comparison, when you wake up, it is like changing the lens of a camera. Prior to waking up, you used the close-up lens to generate your perceptions of reality and of life. After waking up, in contrast, you are able to use a wide angle, or panoramic, lens to view life, giving you an entirely new and expanded perspective.

Another analogy is a television. Waking up is like living your whole life with access to only one channel, and then suddenly being able to access channels that were unavailable to you before. Waking up gives you an expanded awareness and access to a new field of information as you begin to create a whole new playing field for life. When your awareness expands, so do your possibilities. Likewise, so do the depth and quality of questions that you begin to ask once you tap into your newly acquired field of information.

From a practical perspective, consciousness can be thought of as a band of human experience ranging from what are considered lower states of consciousness, such as fear or guilt, to higher states of consciousness, such as love or happiness. Your state of consciousness impacts both how you feel and how you experience life. For example, if you are in a lower state of consciousness, you tend to feel more negatively about life and your experience of life, or what is happening in your external reality, is typically undesirable. Conversely, when you are in a higher state of consciousness, you characteristically feel positive and optimistic about life, and your experience of life is much more favorable. The key here is that your state of consciousness dictates both how you feel and also how you experience your external reality.

From a more metaphysical perspective, some people refer to the expansion of consciousness as the ability to tap into higher dimensions of reality. We live in what is known as the third dimension. This reality has its basis in physical reality, and we use our five senses to define it and navigate through it. In contrast, a higher dimensional reality cannot be experienced using our five senses alone. This is a non-physical or multidimensional – also referred to as spiritual – reality that is experienced with our intuition, feeling, and extrasensory perception. The experience of this reality is much more difficult to share with someone because, unlike the concrete third-dimensional experience of reality, there are no words that correspond to what a person is sensing. For example, the concept of love is not concrete. Love is something that you sense and feel. You can try to explain to someone why you love them or why you love another person, but you can't explain the experience of love itself. Love is not physical or tangible. Love is a frequency and state of being that is experienced, and not something that can be properly described with our limited, three-dimensional vocabulary.

An Expanded Awareness

Waking up brings an expanded sense of awareness and a greater understanding of reality as you start to tap into a larger field of information that was not previously available. Think of someone who has been colorblind their whole life, and then suddenly is able to see the full spectrum of color. Once they can see color, this newly developed sight will alter their previous perspectives and usher in new experiences, definitions, and paradigms associated with being human and with being alive.

In the case of expanded consciousness, the experience of it is not so much what you can see with your physical eyes (at least not in my case), but more about what you are able to sense or feel. This new, intuited field of information completely opens up the aperture on how you process and act on thoughts, and how you view life itself. The following paragraphs detail some effects that are commonly associated with this enhanced awareness.

<u>Heightened Intuition</u>. The universe is always talking to us, although we often don't hear or recognize it when it occurs. When you wake up, your intuition – that inner knowing –

becomes louder and even slower, so that you become more conscious of it and are able to more easily understand what that inner voice is trying to tell you. To put it simply, you became more conscious of and present to your inner guidance system.

Enhanced Discernment. When you wake up, you acquire the ability to more easily differentiate truth from deception and deceit. I like to think of it as an enhanced "BS detector," giving you the ability to hear what people are saying from a more expanded perspective. You can see through the deceptions of false narratives, whether being propagated to the public at large or on a more individual, one-on-one basis.

Frequent Synchronicities and Alignment with the Universe. The universe starts to align itself around you when you start to wake up. In addition to a heightened intuitive sense of awareness, the universe starts talking to you through increased synchronicities. When a message is being communicated to you, you will receive it from various, and often unrelated, sources to be sure that you are listening. Similarly, you may start seeing signs around you more often, such as a frequent sighting of a particular animal, or a repeated set of numbers, everywhere you go. The universe is talking to you because you are more aligned to it and conscious of the communication.

Greater and Deeper Questioning of Everything. Once you are able to see life from an expanded perspective and have access to greater levels of information, your perception of life and "the known" starts to change. This altered perception of reality not only leads you to question the status quo and many of your belief systems, it also begins your deeper level of questioning and the search for the answers to more metaphysical thoughts and queries about life and reality.

Expanded Search for Meaning. Along with your expanded awareness comes the deeper and more enhanced search for more profound meaning and understanding of yourself, reality, and life. Where you may have never delved deep enough or quieted your mind long enough to just "Be," you are now in a place where you begin to ask those life-altering questions of who you are, where you are from, and why you are ultimately here.

<u>Greater Awareness of and Ability to Access Your Personal Power</u>. The awakening process is bittersweet because while it can be an extremely lonely and isolating experience, it can also be a highly empowering experience as you beautifully gain access to your strength and personal power. For many people, including me, the awakening journey thrusts you into a place where, for the first time in your life, you have to navigate life and a new reality all on your own. Though the experience can be very lonely at first, it will guide you to a space where you realize just how powerful, capable, and resilient you truly are.

<u>Increased Human Potential</u>. A higher consciousness level allows you to more easily tap into Source. You are able to remember that you are a divine spiritual being who has a purpose, abilities, and skills. This is where you remember that you are unlimited. You have limitless possibilities and potential.

The awakening process and an expanded awareness happen over time as you start to wake up and are able to integrate the information into your way of being, perceptions, and life. One of the most significant results of an increase in consciousness is that people start to question everything and think about life in ways that they never did before – whereas prior to awakening, the notion of questioning anything in our known worldview or reality would not have even occurred to us. Now, everything is open to scrutiny, questioning, and analysis.

This is where the journey begins. An expanded awareness and a newfound level of critical thinking, enhanced intuition, and questioning are the gateways to entering a "New Human Rite of Passage" for our human family. In the next few chapters,

I will detail the four key stages of the human awakening journey.

Chapter 1 Questions

1. Do you feel like you have had an expansion of consciousness in recent years? If so, what is different in your day-to-day life? What is different in the way you view life and make meaning of it?
2. Have you experienced any of the categories of expanded awareness above? If so, which ones, and how have these changes influenced how you live or view your life?

Chapter 2
The Key Stages of the Awakening Journey
Rite of Passage: *A ritual or experience that marks or constitutes a major milestone or change in a person's life.*
–Merriam-Webster.com

Human rites of passage are prominent in all societies, and play a key role in marking the successful transition through important stages of life. Rites of passage are well known and understood, and are often celebrated through ceremony or other social ritual. These key milestones play an important role in establishing norms and expected behaviors within a social group, helping provide stability and strengthen social bonds within that community. In the Western world, human rites of passage include such major life events as birth, puberty, marriage, having children, and death. Similarly, rites of passage for young people transitioning into adulthood, such as a quinceañera or Bar Mitzvah, are also well known and celebrated in our society. Human rites of passage are foundational, marking major and transitional periods of a human life.

Over the past few years, I have observed a lesser known, but emerging human rite of passage that can be characterized as an expansion of an individual's consciousness. It includes both a heightened sense of awareness and a significant change in human perception, as detailed in Chapter 1. I believe this new human rite of passage is a mass spiritual awakening that is happening to us both individually and as a human collective. While this experience of awakening is not yet widely known, documented, or discussed, I believe that the human awakening journey should be categorized as another major transition in a person's life. Though the awakening process will be unique to each individual, there are definable, yet flexible, stages associated with the experience. The human awakening journey will soon be as recognizable and celebrated as other important human milestones, such as a wedding or the birth of a child.

Waking up is, without a doubt, one of the most life-altering and reality-shattering experiences that a human will ever go through. There is nothing like the experience of this new human rite of passage, which will take you on a journey that will shatter many of your current known knowns, and introduce you to a combination of both disturbing and empowering unknown unknowns.

Although the human awakening journey is currently the path less traveled, I believe that all human beings alive today came to our beautiful planet for that very reason – to wake up. We are here to see through the illusions and manipulation so we can see this reality for what it is and powerfully find ourselves in the process. I believe we are here to remember who we are and discover the power and potential that exists within all of us. There is probably no greater rite of passage than waking up, and I look forward to taking the journey with you. The following chapters detail the stages of the human awakening journey.

Chapter 2 Questions
1. How do you equate the concept of "Waking Up" to a human rite of passage?
2. Why do you think humanity is waking up?

Chapter 3
Awakening Stage 1: The Illumination Stage
"Toto, I've a feeling we're not in Kansas anymore."
—Fleming 1939

    The Illumination Stage of the human awakening journey could also be characterized as the Rebirth Stage. This is the phase of the process where your expanded view of awareness sets in and you first learn and "innerstand" that pretty much everything you have ever been told about what it is to be human, life in general, and how this reality works, may actually not be true. In fact, you uncover that much of what you have been told (a tale still in play) is based on a narrative that enriches the few at the cost of the many. Similarly, you realize that Shakespeare was correct when he said, "All the world's a stage, And all the men and women merely players." (Shakespeare 2.7.139). Additionally, you learn that much of the information that you consume from mass media is a pantomime scripted to shape your view of yourself and of your reality. You begin to realize that you live in what some people call a matrix, and what I like to think of as a prison of perception. Sadly, you begin to understand that this perceptual prison greatly disempowers you, and keeps you playing a very small and limiting game of life. This is the stage where you realize that you actually know very little about who you are, where you are, and why you are here. This is the part of the journey that the world that you have always lived in starts to fade and a new world, based on an entirely new perception of reality, begins to emerge.

Expanded Awareness

An important aspect of this stage is that your new understanding and perception of reality is not something that you can read about, or even understand from another person. Someone or something cannot convince you of this new sense of awareness and any information gleaned from it. This is something that you must intuit on your own. You, and you alone with your expanded awareness, are the only one who will resonate, or not resonate, with new information presented to you. This information, if you are not ready to awaken, will elude you. Even if this new information happens to enter your conscious mind, it won't stay there long, because it will have no meaning to you or context you can draw from. Awakening is truly a higher dimensional experience that coincides with a new heightened intuitive ability.

Greater Discernment

A greater sense of discernment is also a key feature of this stage. On the path of your awakening journey, you gain an enhanced ability to think more critically. As an example, before waking up, when I heard something on the news that I wanted to investigate, I would actually go to Wikipedia to do "research." (Don't laugh!) Often, I would go there and discover that the topic I was investigating was one that had been labeled as a conspiracy theory. Once I read those words, my research and interest in the topic were over. If Wikipedia defined the topic as a conspiracy theory, then indeed, it must be true. It didn't occur to me to investigate beyond what I had uncovered because I was in a hypnotic, autopilot way of being. I was unconsciously and mind-numbingly comfortable letting someone do the thinking for me. In contrast, with my newly enhanced sense of discernment and expanded consciousness, I no longer took information at face value. I examined all information with a critical lens and a fresh perspective embodied by my new sense of acumen and clear-sightedness.

Synchronistic Alignment

Synchronicity is also an element associated with the first stage of the awakening journey. My personal experience with this stage was very much rife with synchronicity. Not only did I receive affirmations from the universe through songs I heard or a repeating pattern of numbers that maintained a presence in my consciousness, I felt like I was strongly guided and nudged towards information that the universe wanted me to know on subjects that I previously knew nothing about. I would acquire information on these subjects from multiple yet unrelated activities. For example, I could be watching my son play sports, reading a book on history, or listening to music on the way to work – and I would receive the exact same message. No matter what activity I was engaged in, I was led down a particular path towards information that the universe wanted to disclose to me. Synchronistic alignment with the universe and the intuitive impulse to actually listen and understand are a profound aspect of this stage.

You Are Alone

One other characteristic of this stage is that you learn quickly that you are often alone in your new insights, and that you must brave your new reality independently. You realize that although you have started the awakening journey, many of your friends and loved ones are not yet there. As an example, I tried to talk to friends about my new insights, and they immediately changed the subject. It's not that they were being rude. It was more that they simply could not hear what I was trying to say. Remember my television channel analogy? When trying to talk to people who are not yet awake, the communication is not received because you are on one channel and they are on another. In short, people who are not ready for this type of information won't hear you because it will have no meaning to them. People who are not yet awake will not have the context that will allow this new information to cement in their consciousness. In this stage, you realize that most of the people that you interact with on a daily basis are functioning in a different reality. They are living within the bounds of the information that you were once constrained by, while you are having a completely different experience of life. This new incompatibility with the people that you love the most is probably the hardest part of the journey, though it does get better with time.

Your Dark Night of the Soul

Waking up can be a traumatic experience because it shatters the core of your reality and leaves you struggling with what to do next. What do you do when you realize that your perception of reality may be based on a false narrative? What do you do when you can't really even talk about it with your closest allies and support system? This stage can leave you scared, hopeless, and feeling isolated. This is the part of the process where you realize that you have perhaps entered what is often referred to as a Dark Night of the Soul. The dark night is defined as "a collapse of perceived meaning in life … an eruption into your life of a deep sense of meaninglessness." (eckharttolle.com 2024) This dark night sets in as you begin to watch the structure of your life, with all the associated meaning you have given to the life you have built, start to mercilessly yet divinely crumble all around you, leaving you confused, lost, and alone. This can be a difficult stage as you try to integrate your expanded state of consciousness and new state of being, but it can also be the start of a very empowering process. This is the stage where you become aware, maybe for the first time, of your inner strength and your own personal power. This stage starts you on the path of a journey that is well worth taking.

Stage 1 of the awakening journey meets you with a profoundly unquenchable thirst for knowledge. Once you start peeling the onion of truth, you have a difficult time actually thinking about anything else. At this point in the process, you know just enough to be dangerous, but you undoubtedly have more questions than answers: What is this reality anyways? What is truth? Who am I? Where am I? Who or what can I trust? You have an unrelenting need to know more. This is the part of the awakening journey that leads you right into the next stage of the process. This is where you enter the next stage – Stage 2 – that I like to call the Rabbit Hole Stage.

Chapter 3 Questions

1. What was your first "light bulb" moment when you realized that the world is not what you thought it was? What was your most important discovery when you first woke up?
2. What kind of synchronicities did you experience when you started to wake up? How did you know that you were beginning to be more connected to the universe?
3. What was your experience when trying to discuss what you were sensing and uncovering about our world with your loved ones? What was their reaction? Did you experience the feeling of being alone? Did you gain value from having to stand alone in your new truths?
4. Did you go through a Dark Night of the soul? What did you find out that was the most reality shattering for you? Did you start to find your power in your Dark Night?

Chapter 4
Awakening Stage 2: The Rabbit Hole Stage

"This your last chance. After this there is no turning back. You take the blue pill; the story ends. You wake up in your bed and believe what you want to. You take the red pill, you stay in Wonderland, and I show you how deep the rabbit hole goes. Remember, all I'm offering is the truth. Nothing more."

–The Matrix

The Rabbit Hole Stage, which could be dubbed the Tinfoil Hat Stage, is a stage in the awakening process where you start your quest for truth. You have started to process and internalize the realization that much of your lifelong knowns that you considered self-evident, common knowledge, and unquestionable, are based on a narrative that is mostly likely not true. In fact, you begin to realize that humanity may have been, and is still being, purposely misled. You realize that you need to unlearn everything you have ever known so that you can create a new foundation for your life that is based in truth – not truth that you learn from other people, and not truth that you hear on the news. You need to build a foundation for your life that is based on a new truth – a truth crafted from your new heightened intuition and enhanced discernment. But where do you start? Where do you look? This is where you begin turning over every rock, looking for answers. This is where you happily jump down every rabbit hole you can find, looking for truth.

Put On Your Tinfoil Hat

When I think of going down the rabbit hole, I visualize Alice from *Alice in Wonderland* heading into the unknown, eager to see what she finds. When you begin your journey to find truth, one of the first things you realize is that there are many coexisting versions of realities at play all around you. Before waking up, regrettably, I paid very little attention to current events or the news. If I did want to find out more about a particular topic, I would typically watch my local news or tune into a more national news outlet such as Cable News Network (CNN) or Fox News. I was familiar with mainstream media but I was unaware of, and had no exposure to, independent or alternative media until I started my journey down the rabbit hole searching for answers.

Finding alternative media greatly opens the aperture, and gives you access to new information and alternative points of view that you will not find in any mainstream news outlet. I began to understand why people on the quest for truth use the term "rabbit hole," because there are not only an innumerable variety of topics to explore, but also layers upon layers of information associated with each subject. You could spend months going down one rabbit hole to research a specific topic, and not even scratch the surface. You discover that trying to research and absorb this newfound information is like peeling an onion with unending layers. As you start to understand one aspect, you quickly recognize that the topic is multilayered, and one piece of information leads you to examine another. Then you realize that you have developed even more questions which, sadly, outnumber the ones you have answered. Your rabbit hole research journey often leaves you mentally, physically, and emotionally exhausted.

Alternative media will give you information on topics that mainstream media calls conspiracy theories. A conspiracy theory is "a theory that explains an event or set of circumstances as the result of a secret plot by usually powerful conspirators." (Merriam-Webster.com) Stumbling upon a different narrative associated with well-known conspiracy theories in the alternative media universe is a fascinating part of the journey, because you start to understand why some people actually believe in the theories that most of humanity has dismissed as not credible – because mainstream media has branded them as such. Then you find that you actually start believing in many of these conspiracy theories yourself.

But why? Why is it that you now start to question theories that you easily dismissed as nonsense in the past? For me, the answer was disturbing.

First, one of the main reasons I never questioned subjects labeled as a conspiracy theory is because they held little interest for me. If the topic didn't affect me personally, I honestly just didn't care about it. Then, if the topic did pique my interest, as soon as I saw it labeled as a conspiracy theory, I looked no further. I assumed it was made-up fantasy and simply dismissed it. (Regrettably, I fell prey to many other labels used by mainstream media to derail the public from looking deeper at a forbidden subject). Next, I didn't question the topic further because when I did try to do any research, I used mainstream resources such as television news or internet searches, and those led me to the same single place of truth, which ended my search. The bottom line was that I only had access to a single, coordinated mainstream narrative, because I had not yet been introduced to alternative news sources which could broaden my research.

Finally, you start to reexamine some conspiracy theories as plausible concepts because they are not the only topics discussed on alternative media. In fact, you find that some very foundational concepts that we have grown up knowing as unquestionable key truths are not true. One such example is that we have been taught from childhood something is real if we see it and experience it with our five senses – or "We must see it to believe it." But in quantum physics, we learn that we create our reality with our thoughts, emotions, and actions. Unlike what we have been taught most of our lives, you learn that in order to manifest something in your reality, you must "Create it to see it."

After you begin the awakening journey, your synchronistic alignment with the universe leads you to non-mainstream data, and your enhanced discernment gives you the ability to analyze the information you find through a much clearer lens. This new lens helps a lot when you are thrust into the world of alternative media, which is built on a completely different set of knowns, and has its own set of commonly held beliefs and norms that create a very different version of reality. In fact, you find yourself living in a version of reality that is vastly different from the one you experienced most of your life. Truth be told, you realize that if you were to go back to your normal life and old worldview and try to discuss your newfound reality with your friends, they would not understand. Moreover, you would undoubtedly be considered one of those crazy tin foil hat people who stupidly believes in nonsense. **This is where you begin to realize the impact that perception truly has on reality, and that there are multiple versions of reality coexisting in our beautiful world today.**

An Alternate Reality

One of the most profound parts of waking up is seeing that reality truly is based in human perception. Growing up, I knew that people had different value and belief systems that shaped their particular ways of being, including habits, career choices, and affiliations with various groups and political parties. A variety of value and belief systems among the human population is definitely understandable, as people are influenced by a myriad of external and internal factors. What I didn't realize until I started to wake up, however, was that perception drives reality. For example, people who are born into a wealthy family often have abundant mindsets throughout their lives. In contrast, children who are born into a family where money, food, and material possessions are not readily available, often develop a scarcity mindset that is also carried into adulthood and maintained throughout their lives. The difference between these two types of individuals in this scenario is their perception of what is possible. For one, wealth is abundant, easy to obtain, and completely possible. For the other, wealth is elusive, and not perceived as possible.

Why is this important? Because if perception influences reality, you can see why human beings are so divided, and view the world so differently. In the past few years, people in the United States have become extremely polarized, and I realized that I was beginning to understand why. From my vantage point, I observed at least three versions of reality in America, and I could now even pinpoint why that was. For example, if you are a Democrat and get your news from a left-leaning news outlet, then you are in one reality. In contrast, if you are a Republican and get your news from right-leaning news outlets, you are in a second, vastly different reality. Lastly, if your source of news is gathered from watching alternative media, you are in yet another reality. **These divergent, coexisting realities are unfortunately becoming much more acute with the inception of artificial intelligence that unknowingly puts people in a type of echo chamber that continually reinforces their view of reality – a reality that is absent of other possible points of view.**

This is crazy when you think about it. I grew up thinking that news outlets were a credible source of information whose job was not to offer an opinion, but instead, provide the public with facts and data from which people could form their own. It was my understanding that the media was unbiased, and served the public as our arbiters of truth. Sometimes I honestly think that we Americans have forgotten that our public servants work for us. We live in a constitutional republic, and we elect leaders to manage our country on our behalf. The media was established to be our eyes and ears, providing us with important, factual information about our government, leaders, and country.

But do they? Does the mainstream media, regardless of the slant – left or right – provide us with unbiased, truthful information? Do they even provide us with useful information? Or, do they simply parrot a narrative that serves to shape our reality? Is that possible? At this point in the journey, you actually realize that this is most likely true. You begin to comprehend that mainstream media is not really reporting accurate news. Instead, much of the news that mainstream media reports is not only sensationalized, it is actually fictitious. Most news outlets parrot a methodically scripted narrative instead of providing us with unbiased facts about a topic.

The information that you uncover about the mainstream media and its role in shaping reality by parroting a false narrative is just one example of a multitude of reality-shattering breakthroughs you have as you continue your journey down the rabbit hole. Your thirst for knowledge and research fragments so many of your belief systems and leaves you questioning many of your previously cemented core truths. As you go further down the path, searching for truth on alternative media platforms, you unfortunately soon discover that some alternative platforms are also parroting a false narrative in order to influence your perception. UGH! "Why is it so darn hard to find truth?" you ask yourself. "Who and what can be trusted?" These are just some of the questions that this stage of the process leaves you asking.

At this point in the journey, you begin to slow down your research, and you start to synthesize the vast amount of data you have amassed from your journey down the rabbit hole. **Probably the most substantial takeaway from this phase of the awakening process is that you begin to understand that truth is, in fact, very hard to come by, and that you must begin to rely on your newly enhanced instincts, intuition, and discernment to determine your own version of truth, and shape what will become your newfound reality.**

Before you can begin to put all of your questioning aside, however, you realize that all the data you have amassed has led you to the part of your journey where your questions about life and reality become more expanded and even philosophical. You comprehend that before you can even begin to construct a new version of reality for yourself, you have to first understand the concept of reality itself. In addition to examining reality, you begin a deeper search for the meaning of life and its purpose in general. You acquire an unquenchable and unrelenting thirst to understand the more esoteric, metaphysical aspects of life and of reality. This is the point in the journey that you truly begin to examine deeper truths such as, "Who am I?" "Where am I?" and even "Why am I?" This is the part where you enter the next stage of the awakening journey – Stage 3 – which is called The Data Synthesis and Analysis Stage.

Chapter 4 Questions

1. What was your experience going down the rabbit hole? What was the most significant unknown unknown that you found?
2. Were you aware of independent or alternative media before you started waking up? How did you feel when you discovered an entirely new perspective on current events from these alternative news sources?
3. Do you view conspiracy theories differently than you did before? If so, how, and what changed your mind? What surprised you the most about what you learned regarding conspiracy theories?
4. What sources do you use at this point of your journey when looking for truth?
5. What surprised you the most about your rabbit hole deep dive?

Chapter 5
Awakening Stage 3: The Data Synthesis and Analysis Stage

"A man's mind, stretched by new ideas, may never return to its original dimensions."

–Oliver Wendell Holmes

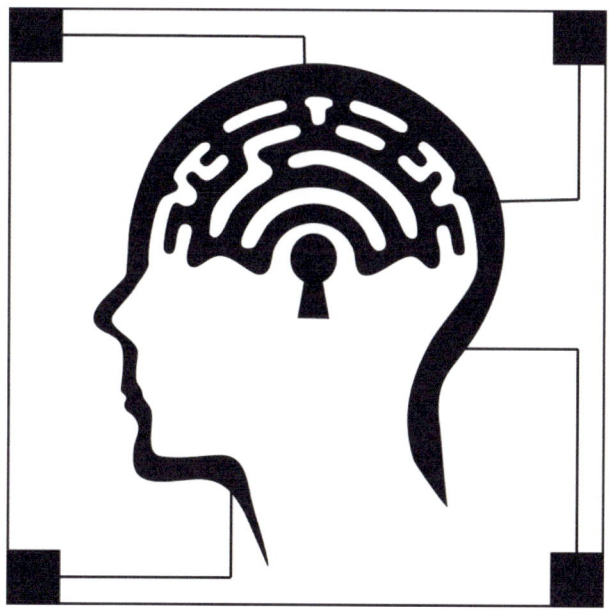

At this important stage, you have fully processed and internalized the fact that you have been living a life based on a false narrative about the purpose of life and the nature of our reality. Your view of reality and the meaning that you have associated with the life you have built have shattered. You find that you have entered a void. You are in a reality no man's land of sorts. Moreover, you find that you are in your new environment – your new reality – mostly by yourself. What do you do now?

I call this phase of the awakening journey The Data Synthesis and Analysis Stage, but you could also call it The Deep Thoughts Stage. At this point, you start to ask the deeper, more metaphysical questions about the meaning of life and reality itself. This is the part of the process where you must step back and become the observer of the reality that humanity lives within, so that you can begin to make sense of it all. This is when you truly have to take the emotion out of all you have learned, and approach your data synthesis, and analysis of that data, with a sense of detachment. Let's face it, finding out that most of what you have been taught and have aligned your belief systems around is based on a false narrative – a narrative that most people still believe is true – can be traumatic. You can easily find yourself losing all sense of purpose as you try to function in two realities. You still have to pay the bills, take care of family, and go to school or work. You still have to live out your roles as a child, a parent, a spouse, a friend, an employee, a boss, etc. The purpose you serve and the roles you play in your old reality still exist. You still have to show up and participate every day.

At the same time, you must show up for your new reality. You have an unquenchable thirst to understand. You want to give some meaning to your life, a life that will remain in a void, until you have enough information to build a new life on the secure foundation of your newly defined truth. Even though you are experiencing some very real feelings as a result of all you have learned – sadness, loss, fear, hopelessness – you know that these feelings need to be compartmentalized so that you can live in both worlds, at least until you can create a new reality that combines them seamlessly.

A Higher State of Consciousness

The new reality that you are living in is based beyond our three-dimensional perception of reality. Similarly, you learn that this reality is not bound or limited by our three-dimensional state of consciousness. In other words, this new version of reality is experienced from a higher state of consciousness and from a different, higher frequency than you experience when you are tapped into your old reality. Simply put, your new reality is on a different channel than your old one. Why is this important? **Because your higher state of consciousness allows**

you to not only ask the deeper and more esoteric questions regarding our life and our reality, it also allows you to synthesize and understand the answers that you begin to formulate. Additionally, a higher state of consciousness gives you the discernment to be able to separate fact from fiction. **This becomes critical as you move through your awakening process and learn (spoiler alert) that the truth about life and reality is solely dependent on what you decide it is about. It is all up to you.** Being in a higher state of consciousness, however, ensures you have the proper tools to help you make these key decisions that will shape the rest of your life.

The Questions You Ask

You begin to ask yourself many different questions following your innumerable trips down the rabbit hole, especially because your journey exposes many hidden truths about life and how our world actually works. These truths are vastly different from what you were taught and previously understood.

For me, this was an intellectually exhausting part of the journey because I could not use my logical mind to ask my questions or find answers. Although I grew up in a society that greatly values intellect as well as the use of mental strategies to solve problems and function in life, these tried-and-true strategies would not work for me now. Instead, I had to stay tapped into a higher frequency and a higher state of consciousness – more spiritual than mental – to not only understand but to also synthesize the information in such a way that I could fully embody. Intellectual understanding of a subject, I found, is vastly different than the spiritual embodiment of that knowledge. The latter is experienced as a part of your everyday life and reality. This knowledge, once embodied, becomes a part of who you are. It becomes second nature.

The reason I lightheartedly characterize this stage of the journey as The Deep Thoughts Stage is because I have always been one of those people who tend to ponder those deeper, meaning-of-life questions. In fact, my close friends have always playfully referred to my habit as "Deep Thoughts with Fran." Although I paid little attention to current events or to things happening around me in my physical reality, I did spend a lot of my life searching for meaning and trying to fully understand my spiritual reality. I studied human nature and deeper concepts such as how humanity influences or does not influence reality.

Even though I was a deep thinker on the more metaphysical topics of life, trying to *even* formulate all the questions that I wanted answered was challenging. This is where the process gets interesting because you realize that you have started to think, or perhaps perceive, multidimensionally. This is difficult to explain in words, but when you are trying to ask and answer a specific question, you become aware of the fact that you see it from multiple vantage points. On one hand, you can see both the question and the answer from a three-dimensional, or physical, perspective. On the other hand, you realize that you can see the question and the answer from a higher dimensional, or spiritual, point of view. For example, when trying to answer the question "Who Am I?" people characteristically go down the list of three-dimensional descriptors, such as

- I am a female
- I am an American
- I am Caucasian
- I am tall
- I am a mom
- I am married
- I am an athlete
- I work in the defense industry
- I am a dog lover
- I am an independent political voter
- I am kind
- I am an introvert
- I am a human

The three-dimensional list of characteristics that define who you are can be endless when you use the five senses and

categories that human beings often use to describe themselves. In contrast, when trying to answer the question of "Who Am I?" from a higher-dimensional or spiritual perspective, you answer it more metaphysically using descriptors such as:
- I am a spirit in a body having a human experience
- I am from Source
- I am consciousness
- I am a point of awareness

This list can be unending as well.

The key point here is that you become conscious that you are thinking, questioning, and analyzing from a higher state of consciousness. This is important because you discover that trying to synthesize and analyze all of the data you have uncovered will not be as easy as you thought it would be. Instead, with your expanded consciousness, and with the multidimensional nature of your ability to process information, you realize that answers to even basic questions can have a myriad of responses. Moreover, you realize that many answers, though different, can also be accurate, depending on whether they are being answered from a three-dimensional or higher-dimensional perspective.

Regardless of the complexity of this process, you do finally begin to formulate many of the questions that will give you a better understanding of who and where you are, so you can begin to build a life grounded in your newly-acquired version of truth. The number of questions can be boundless, but here are some of the most common that people begin to postulate at this point in the awakening process:

Who am I?
- Beyond what I have been told, who and what is the person (or spirit) living my life?
- Where did I come from?
- Where am I going?

Where am I?
- Where is my consciousness really?
- Am I really on Earth?
- Am I in a simulation or a game?

Why am I?
- Why am I here?
- What is my purpose?
- What is my life about?

How do I perceive reality?
- Why is human perception of reality being controlled and manipulated?
- Who is manipulating our reality and to what end?
- How long has human perception been manipulated?
- How are we being manipulated?
- Who can I trust?
- What is real?
- Why is my perception (my mind) so important?

Do I live in a matrix?
- What does it mean to live in a matrix?
- Are the systems (educational, pharmaceutical, banking, financial, etc.) that we live and function within designed to enslave us?
- Is the matrix a sort of prison for our minds?
- Is the movie *The Matrix* a documentary? (Ha!)
- What is the nature of my physical reality?
- Is Earth real, or do we live in a simulation?
- Do we live in a hologram?
- Is this all just a dream?

What is the nature of my spiritual reality?
- Is everything that I have been told from a spiritual perspective true?
- What happens when I die?

- Do I have a spiritual mission?
- How do I connect to Source?
- How does the multidimensional aspect of myself work?
- Do I have powers and abilities that I am not aware of?

There certainly is a vast amount of information to unpack after your questions have been formulated and you have started to develop the multifaceted answers to each one. If you were to create a mind map of the data points you have amassed, your picture would look like a very complicated spider web. The threads of data are multilayered and vast; however, most of the topics can be put in two major categories.

Most of the questions and new insights are from two specific root sources and two key main themes. **Both provide critical insights into previously unknown unknowns. The first theme is related to what you have learned – that you didn't know before – about the world and the reality that you grew up in. The second theme involves key insights and foundational information about your world and reality – also unknown to you until now – that are extremely important and empowering.**

<u>Key Theme #1: Our World Is Not What We Think It Is</u>

The first key theme is the concept that the world that we grew up in is different from what we thought it was. **We have based many of our beliefs systems, core truths, and self-evident knowns on a false narrative.** The following is a high-level summary of some (though not all) of the key insights about the world and reality that you grew up in:

1. Much of what you have been told, and thus the concepts that you have built your life on, are based on a false narrative which enriches the few at the cost of the many. Most of what we have been told and taught about ourselves and our history is not completely true.

2. There is a vast amount of critical information about our reality, our history, and humanity itself that has been purposely withheld from the public.
3. Humans think they are being educated when, in fact, they are being indoctrinated.
4. Perception influences reality, and human perception is being manipulated to its detriment.
5. Humanity is purposely kept in lower states of consciousness, and humans live in a low vibrational state. Fear is an easy, and commonly used, way to lower human vibration.
6. Humanity lives within a vast array of systems (e.g. financial, pharmacological, educational) that are disempowering and equally detrimental to its growth, well-being, and ability to expand.
7. Humanity has been programmed to play a very limited game of life that is based in survival, even though human beings have the tools within them to thrive.
8. Humanity is being purposely divided into groups (color, race, religion, politics) to create disharmony.
9. Humans are being distracted externally (e.g. entertainment, technology, social media, etc.) so that they **never find their true internal power, which can only be found when they focus their attention inwardly. The notion that "The kingdom of God is within you" (King James Version Luke 17:21) is not a metaphor. This is the truth.**

<u>Key Theme #2 – We Are Much More Powerful Than We Think We Are.</u>
<u>We Just Didn't Understand the Rules nor Have the Tools</u>
The second key theme is based on the notion that human beings are much more powerful and are in much more control of this reality than we were taught and programmed to believe.

These concepts, which have not been taught to us nor are readily available to us, contain knowledge and wisdom that will empower us. I consider these concepts to be rules and tools that can be used to empower you when you begin to powerfully create a new strategy and a game of life that will be well worth playing:

1. Humanity is waking up.
    a. Humanity is raising its frequency and increasing the level of its consciousness. Humanity is waking up individually and collectively.
    b. The activation of your deoxyribonucleic acid (DNA) is an important part of the awakening process.
2. Your energetic and spiritual connection to Source is paramount.
    a. The frequency of your body and level of consciousness is a direct result of your ability or inability to access your connection to Source or your intuitive voice. The higher your frequency and level of consciousness, the easier it is to access Source and your intuitive voice.
    b. The stronger your connection to Source, the more effectively you will be able to traverse your reality, create a life you love, find your purpose, and fulfill your life's mission.
3. Our nonphysical, or spiritual, world is just as real as our physical world. We are multidimensional beings with a spirit, though we have been taught to identify with and focus on our physicality.
4. Human beings have many more abilities (telepathic, psychic, claircognizant) than we have been taught. We will be able to access them as we raise our frequency and start to focus our attention inwardly.

5. We are one. We are connected to everything and everyone.
6. Life is not happening to us. We co-create this entire reality.
7. Consciousness is King and one of the most powerful tools that we have at our disposal.
8. We create this reality with our conscious and subconscious minds, both of which play important roles in manifesting our reality.
    a. We use our conscious mind to co-create our reality through the intentional use of our thoughts, emotions and actions. Being mindful of your thoughts is a critical part of manifesting a life you want.
    b. Our subconscious mind is mostly habitual, and is populated with unconscious programs that we have been accumulating since birth.
        i. There are publicly available tools and programs that can be used to overwrite the unconscious programs that dominate your subconscious mind.
        ii. It is critical to manage the content that you consume (e.g. negative news and violent movies) because your subconscious mind does not know the difference between what is real and what is fantasy.
9. Your frequency level (i.e. the level at which you vibrate) is critically important to your overall well-being.
    a. The frequency of your body dictates the level of your consciousness. The higher your frequency, the higher and more expanded is your level of consciousness. The lower your frequency, the lower your level of consciousness.

    b. The frequency of your body has a role in your ability to manifest what you want. You will not be able to manifest anything unless you are an energetic match for what you are trying to create.
10. Love is the most powerful force in the universe. Unconditional love reigns supreme.
11. You have the ability to heal yourself.
    a. Your health is directly attributable to your thoughts, your level of consciousness, and your frequency.
    b. Your health also relies on the health and well-being of your energy body.
12. Light is more powerful than darkness. No matter what is happening in the world, light will always illuminate darkness.
13. Knowledge is power.
    a. The more you know, the more effective you will be at managing your perception of reality.
    b. Knowledge greatly expands your access to possibilities and the fulfillment of your potential.
14. Mother Earth
    a. Our planet is conscious, and we are deeply and energetically connected to Mother Earth.
    b. The frequency of our planet is increasing, which is raising the frequency of our bodies as well.

The Data Synthesis and Analysis Stage is an important part of your awakening journey because it gives you the knowledge, wisdom, and tools to begin to rebuild your life based in truth as you have begun to define it. For the first time in your life, you truly are in control and have become the conscious driver and shaper of your life and of your destiny. You are in a good place where you have asked many of the questions that resulted from your awakening, and you have acquired some of your answers. You have examined the two key themes associated with the analysis of the data that you gathered. You can clearly see the world you grew up in and understand your old reality from an expanded state of consciousness. Most importantly, you are now armed with both the rules and the tools to successfully navigate your new world. You are ready to begin your new life, but where do you start?

    You are at a very empowering part of your journey. Your canvas is blank and waiting for you to craft a new story and give renewed purpose to a life that you are excited and equipped to build. You are now ready to enter the next phase of your awakening journey – Stage 4, "The Choice Stage."

Chapter 5 Questions

1. Did you find it hard to piece together all that you uncovered during your rabbit hole research so that you could make sense of it all?
2. Did you notice that you were beginning to think multidimensionally when you tried to synthesize the data that you found during your research?
3. What did you find out about your old world that surprised you the most? What troubled you the most?
4. Did you find any information about our reality, or about your innate power, that surprised and empowered you?
5. Did you ask any questions that are not listed in this chapter?

Chapter 6
Awakening Stage 4: The Choice Stage
"Once you make a decision, the universe conspires to make it happen."
—Ralph Waldo Emerson

Although Stage 4 is the last – for now – stage of your awakening journey, in many ways it is actually the start of a powerful new chapter in your life. You realize that you are living in two clearly definable realities or, stated differently, two distinct worlds. The first reality is the world that you grew up in, and the one in which most of humanity resides in and resonates with. This is the world based on a perception of reality that you now know to be false, and one that you no longer resonate with and have started to outgrow. The second reality is your new world based on a newly defined perception of reality, acquired as a result of your awakening and of your avid research efforts. You have your feet firmly planted in both your new and old worlds and are trying to determine where to go from here.

Your next step begins with some soul searching and the process of asking yourself a few very important questions. You realize that you are still living in a no man's land when you have to, and even want to, function in your old world. You still must take care of yourself and your loved ones. You still have the day-to-day responsibilities of making a living and putting food on the table. You still have to meet all of your physical and financial needs, be an active participant in that world, and contribute to your family and society.

 More importantly, you still want to be a part of that world. You still want to stay connected to friends and to your family. You still want to laugh and have fun with the people that you love. You still want to find joy and meaning in your life within this world. You still want to feel normal and remain connected to all you have ever known.

 But you are not the same. You have changed dramatically as a result of your awakening. You can't fully go back, but you also don't know how to go forward. How do you find balance between your new and old paradigms of reality? How do you find peace? How can you begin to integrate your new awakened insights into your old world? How can you merge your worlds so that you can fully move forward and begin your new life? Where do you start? Your new journey begins with a powerful new line of questioning.

A New Set of Questions

 The keys to your success in defining a new future and closing the divide between your two worlds is to remember all of the rules and tools you have learned through your research that you can now actively apply to building a new life that you love. Though you have been consciously, or unconsciously, playing a game of life that you created based on your then-perception of reality, you now actually have the tools to redefine your life and consciously create a new path designed from a higher state of consciousness. Your canvas is waiting for you to breathe new life onto it, and create an entirely new life for yourself. You are ready to leave the void that you have been living in between your two worlds, and use the power of your conscious mind to create a new story for yourself and your life. All old definitions of your life, and what is and is not possible for you, fall away. You stand empowered.

The void that you currently live in holds much power and can be a conduit to your next step. The void is an empty space which has no beginning and no end. In the void, there is no memory of a past, nor anticipation of a future. There is only the beautiful present moment, which is the most powerful place from which to choose and to create something new. In the present moment, you are no longer afflicted with any limitations from the past that you or other people have placed on you, or on what is possible for you. There is no past perception of who you are and what you are capable of accomplishing. The past no longer has a stranglehold on your future. The future can be created free from any limitations imposed from your past. You are in the sweet spot of the empty space that is associated with the present moment, where you get to powerfully decide who you want to be and what your life is ultimately about. You are in a place where you get to consciously choose both who you are and where you are going. You get to create a new vision, purpose, and game for your life. You are in complete control.

Writing a new plan for yourself and for your life starts with three fundamental questions. **These three foundational questions will act as the roots for your new life, and will serve as a grounding mechanism and source from which all other decisions will be made:**

Who am I?
Where am I?
Why am I?

Who Am I?

We have often heard people talk about finding themselves, and this has always intrigued me. Looking back, I realize that I associated finding oneself with an external endeavor, where people search the world for answers that will help shape their personal realities, and provide some perceived clarity of who they are.

Your awakened endeavor to define "Who Am I?" however, will be quite different. This is not an exercise to look externally for a definition of who you are. Instead, this is an internal pursuit where you actively get to powerfully **decide** who you want to be. The fact that you are proactively and consciously making a decision is an important distinction, because you are choosing a course for your life that is no longer reactive to anything that is happening externally. You are in a position of power. You are in a co-creative position of choosing.

The most important part of choosing "Who Am I" is to be sure that you are choosing from a higher state of consciousness. You will no longer be defining yourself in terms of your three-dimensional physical reality. Instead, you will be defining yourself from a higher dimensional perspective where you are no longer a human **doing** – you are actually moving into a world where you are a human **being**.

The main task is to **decide who you want to be in the world**. You are deciding what is possible through you and through your Being. You are no longer define yourself as a person physically with statements like "I am tall," "I live in Virginia," "I am a professional," etc. Instead, you powerfully define yourself in terms of who you are Being, like "I am powerful," "I am light," "I am fearless," etc.

The key to powerfully defining who you are is to consciously define yourself, not as a person, but as a Potential. You define yourself by consciously choosing what you want to bring into this world through you, as a result of who you are Being. Defining yourself as a human Being makes a powerful statement to the universe and places you in a very empowered position.

Where Am I?

"Where Am I?" is another important question to ask and to consciously decide. Typically, when you think of the concept of "Where am I?" you think of a geographical or geospatial question. You answer it from the perspective of where you are physically located at a point in time on our planet.

Some people who are starting to wake up also think of the concept of "Where Am I?" from a deeper and more esoteric perspective. Do we actually live on a physical planet, or in some sort of a computer-generated simulation? Some who do believe that we live on a physical planet question whether or not the earth is actually round, or is it flat? All of these are great questions and ones that I have also pondered, but not what I am referring to with "Where Am I?"

"Where Am I?" is not a question that can be answered from a three-dimensional perspective. The answer to this question is not rooted in physicality. Instead, this is a metaphysical question, and must be considered from a higher dimensional state of consciousness. You are asking a more foundational question: **"Where is My Consciousness?"**

Understanding where you are physically is important; however, asking yourself "Where is my consciousness?" is much more fundamental. This question is more metaphysical and gets to the root of some even more foundational questions such as:

"How does this reality work?"
"What laws are associated with this reality?"
"What are the physics of this reality? "

It ultimately begs the important question: Why is my consciousness here in the first place?

Answering these important questions positions you in a place of great power, because it gives you vital insight into how to navigate this reality so you can consciously co-create within it. Think of an owner's manual of a car: It tells you how and when to change your oil, and provides information on troubleshooting when your car is malfunctioning. Similarly, understanding the laws of physics that pertain to your consciousness is how you will be able to co-create within this reality. Understanding "Where Am I?" from a consciousness perspective is the instrument that will allow you to manifest all that you desire into this world. More importantly, it is the mechanism by which you will be able to bring to life your new

Being after you have consciously answered the question of "Who Am I?"

"Where is My Consciousness?" leads you to ponder an even more foundational question: "What is the purpose of this reality?" When you wake up in the morning and open your eyes, you know you are somewhere. Your consciousness is plugged into this reality, and you see a big beautiful world all around you. You know you are somewhere, but what you don't know is why you are there. What you do not know, but need to determine, are the answers to a few key questions, such as:

"What is my consciousness doing here?"
"What is the purpose of this reality?"
"Ultimately, why is humanity here?"

Unpacking the important question of "Where Am I?" helps you on your journey as you learn to navigate this reality, so you can work within its laws and use the power of your conscious mind to co-create and manifest within it. Additionally, determining why your consciousness is here and defining your perception of the ultimate purpose of this reality are also critical steps to move forward and build a new life that you love. After working through the critical question of "Where Am I?" you are left with a third and equally important question to be answered: "Why Am I?"

Why Am I?

In my life, I have often pondered "Who Am I?" but it wasn't until recently that I first asked myself "Why Am I?" Once I started asking this question, I immediately began to notice the power it contained. "Why Am I?" also must be answered from a higher dimensional state of consciousness. This question gets to the heart of defining your mission and your ultimate purpose for Being.

Although questions like these have been asked by many people all over the world, it is not until you ask this question from a higher state of consciousness that you really start to find its power. At this point in your journey, you no longer seek to answer to these questions externally, or by going outside of yourself. Instead, you realize that the answers to these questions are found inside of you. It is an internal pursuit that is best answered by using one of the most powerful resources that you have at your disposal: The best way to answer the question of "Why Am I?" is found by tapping in and exploring the answers from the space of your beautiful heart!

The question "Who Am I?" leaves you with a profound choice, and a knowing of what it is that you plan to Be in this world. It determines what will be possible through you in this reality. It tells the universe what you plan to birth into this world simply by your Beingness. Finding the answer to the question of "Why Am I?" takes that decision to the next level. "Who Am I?" and "Why Am I?" are separate yet complementary decisions. **While defining "Who Am I?" makes a statement about your Beingness in this world, "Why Am I?" puts that decision into powerful action. "Who Am I?" tells the universe what you plan to Be in the world and what is possible through your Beingness. "Why Am I?" tells the universe what specifically you plan to do with your Beingness.**

As an example, someone might choose to define themselves or their Being as a powerful healer. To complement that declaration, that person might define their "Why Am I?" as someone who opens a yoga studio. In this case, the Beingness of a healer manifests as the owner of a yoga studio. Similarly, the Beingness of a healer could also manifest as someone who heals people just by being a good friend, or by serving healthy food to his or her family. The Beingness of a healer can manifest in multiple forms, and be acted on in a variety of ways. The goal in all of this is just to powerfully choose who, where, and why you exist in every moment. The most important aspect is to embody yourself as a human Being.

Bringing It All Together – Integrating Your Two Realities

Why Am I? *Who Am I?* *Where Am I?*

Answering the three fundamental questions "Who Am I?" "Where Am I?" and "Why Am I?" begins to bridge the divide between your old world and your new world. Answering these questions will begin to bring you out of the void and out of your reality no man's land. It will help you merge the two realities that you now live in. How does that happen?

Until this point in your life, you have been playing a game of life that was built around a false impression of who you were, where you were, and why you were. You have been playing the wrong game, even if you were playing it with vigor, and even if you were playing it successfully by all three-dimensional standards. Now you have awakened and have the rules and the tools for how this reality works. You can start building a life that is based in truth – truth as you have defined it. There is much power in this!

There is also power in what you have learned about the way our reality works. Our physical world is manifested into reality by our consciousness, whether we know it or not. We have individually and collectively been manifesting our world, even if we didn't recognize that we were, or understood how our co-creative abilities work. Now, we understand both.

We are here to be co-creators of our world, and we are here to thrive. We are here to build a life that we love, and collectively build a world that is filled with beauty, compassion, and love.

The merging of your old and new worlds starts with claiming your co-creative power, learning more about the physics of this reality, and deciding what you are going to do with the rest of your life. You are not here by accident. You are here for a purpose!

Now that you are awake, you have been afforded the powerful opportunity to choose how you are going to show up in the world. You get to decide who you plan to Be in this world and what is possible through your Beingness. You get to decide how this reality works, and you get to choose how you are going to manifest your Beingness into the world through the appropriate declaration of "Why Am I?" and by taking the physical action to manifest who you are into this reality.

The merging of your two worlds starts with creating a new, consciously created plan for your life. This new plan, and the merging of your two worlds, begin through answering those three foundational questions. Choosing and declaring who you are, where you are, and why you are is the catalyst for the integration of your two worlds and the start of a process towards building a powerful new life for yourself. You are now well on your way.

Chapter 6 Questions

1. Did you find the answers to the questions posed in this chapter to be interesting or empowering?
2. Are you planning on answering these questions? If so, which question are you most excited about answering?
3. What do you think is the major benefit of consciously choosing who you are, where you are, and why you are?
4. Have you ever felt that you were in a reality no man's land? If so, when and how did you get out of it?

Part II

Chapter 7

My Choice: The Start of a New Plan

"A change of world view can change the world viewed."
–Joseph Chilton Pierce

In hindsight, I can pinpoint my awakening in 2020, but I have been waking up my entire life. Seeds of truth and knowing were planted throughout my life, but 2020 was when all of my seeds sprouted.

I believe this to be true for all human beings. We have all had seeds planted in our minds that make us momentarily question what we know and shift our perceptions just a bit. These moments are brief. We often don't really think about them after they happen, and sometimes don't even remember them until we wake up. Once you start waking up, you see how so many events in your life were connected, the result of the universe nudging you to look at things differently and to question your perception of your world and your reality.

You also realize that some of what you are learning about your world are things that you intuitively already knew. In some ways, it feels like what you uncover when you wake up is what you are remembering instead of learning for the first time. The human awakening journey is a combination of learning new truths and remembering information that was always there, but not accessible to you until the frequency of your body shifted and your DNA activated.

My Awakening Journey

My personal awakening was an unintended spiritual awakening that began in 2020. I say "unintended" because I, like most people, had no idea that there was anything that I needed to wake up to. My awakening was not intentional; however, it was profoundly life altering.

Though I didn't understand what was happening at the time, if I had to identify a specific moment when my consciousness started to expand and I started to wake up, it would be while I was watching a televised press briefing given by my American medical leadership. I still vividly remember staring at the television screen and listening to the message being given to the public, and instantly knowing that was being said was not true. In fact, the thought that occurred to me was very clear: "They are lying."

At the time, I didn't really know why I felt that way. I had watched a similar briefing the day before, and listened without questioning the narrative. All I knew after I had my perceptual shift was that I trusted my instincts, and nobody was going to convince me otherwise. Something in me had changed. My perception of reality and my consciousness had expanded. I was starting to wake up.

It is now 2024 and I am still in the process of waking up. While the human awakening journey has a definable beginning, I am not sure that it ever ends. Waking up is an ever-evolving experience with many layers. Once it starts, it can take a lifetime. In fact, I believe that we will continue to evolve until we are no longer on our beautiful planet.

The human awakening journey – this profound rite of passage – does take time. Sometimes I perceive the process as slow, but four years into my journey, my summation of the experience is that it happens quickly. I can't believe how much I have changed in the past four years. Though the foundational structure of my life is the same – I am still married (thank God because I had just gotten remarried to an awesome man in 2019), I am still a mom, I still live in the same house, and I still work in the same industry – I have changed dramatically. I have gone through all of the stages of the awakening journey, and I have done it mostly on my own.

 Looking back, I can't believe how much I have learned and uncovered about my unknown unknowns – some absolutely horrifying and some profoundly empowering – and how the foundation of my reality was completely shattered. I also can't believe how much I have already started to rebuild a new life. Being one of the first in your world to wake up is exceptionally difficult, but I feel that it is also a gift. I strongly believe that all the souls on our planet today are here to wake up. We are all waking up at our own pace and in our own time, but we are all here to evolve into who we were meant to be. I just happen to have started earlier than my loved ones.

There have been many times that I thought I was losing my mind. I tried so hard to explain to my closest support system what I was dealing with, and they tried to understand. They tried to support me, but they just couldn't relate. About two years ago, I gave up talking to them about my journey, and have found other resources as I continued through the process. The good news is that there are many other people out there waking up, and you can find great resources and ways to connect online that not only help grow your research and understanding, but also validate that you have not gone crazy. You have started to wake up. You are not alone. There are others.

Finding other awakened souls online has helped maintain my sanity. I am thankful. This support system also helped me when it was time to make my choice. It helped me walk through the questions outlined in Stage 4 (The Choice Stage) of the awakening journey so that I could also begin to merge my two worlds – my old one and my new one post awakening. This support system also helped me when it was time to define my new reason for being and to create a new life plan that I loved and that gave me profound purpose.

Choosing Between Two Paths

Once you wake up and understand just how powerful you are, you realize that you have a responsibility to manage that power. This starts with consciously managing your thoughts, your emotions, and the actions that you choose to take. It starts by managing your frequency, your attention, your energy, and your conscious mind. It is an awesome responsibility, and one that I take very seriously.

Believe it or not, Stage 4 of my awakening journey was the longest stage for me. I was stuck for a very long time trying to decide where to focus my attention and how to redefine my purpose in this world. I was unsure how to move forward.

For me, the choice came down to choosing between one of two distinct paths: The first path involved putting my energy into righting the wrongs in my old world. I had learned an enormous amount about the world that I was born in, including how it functions and what was happening behind the scenes. I understood much about the manipulation of humanity and had decent insights into the who, what, and why of the situation. I questioned whether I had a responsibility to make sure that other people also knew. Maybe I should start a podcast and become another source of independent information on current events? Maybe I should write a book detailing what I have learned as a warning to my fellow Americans and the rest of humanity? Maybe I should focus my energy on changing all that is wrong in my world?

The second path involved putting my energy behind all the new rules and tools I had learned through my research. I had learned an incredible amount of new information and gained multidimensional knowledge regarding our reality that I could now use to empower myself and help other people. I had learned that there was a purposeful misunderstanding about what it is to be human and how we relate to ourselves, others, and our environment. I wanted others to learn that, too. Maybe that is what I should do? Maybe my role is to create a platform from which humanity could readily find information about themselves, their power, and their potential that would help empower them? Maybe that is my path?

With the two paths laid out in front of me, I spent several months asking myself the following question: If I am, and I know that I am, an infinite, eternal, powerful, abundant being with an unlimited ability to manifest the reality I want, what would I do with all that I have learned? I mean, think about it – if I knew that I actually had the power to empower other humans as they are working through their shift in consciousness and their awakening journey, what would I do? What should I do? What is most needed right now?

    In truth, we need awakened humans working on both paths. We absolutely need people who are working to help educate the public on what is really happening in our world so that they can wake up. When people start to wake up, they will be looking for answers. People will be abundantly thirsty for truth, and they need a place to go. I will forever be grateful for independent media and those who provided the alternative platforms of information I learned from. The people who have chosen this path are rock stars in my book, and a critical part of our collective human awakening journey. There is no question about this. Though the information is hard to hear and can be devasting, we need to hear it. We can't truly be free until we understand what we are dealing with. Understanding the disturbing truth about our reality is important and needed.

    At the same time, we also need people who are providing the educational resources to help us understand our history and the multidimensional nature of our species. We need people who can teach us how to tap into our creator, and how to access the unlimited power and potential within us.

    When examining the choice between these two paths, it became clear to me that I had narrowed my choices down because I had already made at least one decision. Both paths involved a future where I would be assisting other people through their awakening journey. One path would be focused on what is happening in our physical reality – my old world. The other path would be more focused on tapping into our spiritual and multidimensional nature – my new world. Either path, however, involved providing assistance to human beings as they started to wake up. I realized then that my path would be one of helping to assist humanity in the awakening process. I was here to help people transition through this important new human rite of passage.

Tapping Into My Intuition to Make My Decisions

Once I realized I had already made the first key decision associated with my new life, I knew the next step would be answering the three fundamental questions outlined in Stage 4 of the human awakening journey. To fully answer these questions from a higher dimensional and an expanded consciousness perspective, I needed to first tap into my inner guidance system – my intuition.

I am generally able to tap into my intuition when I am by myself and doing something in nature, such as walking outside or exercising. I am also able to access my intuition and my higher self when I am commuting to and from work, or if I am meditating. My intuitive downloads typically happen when I am performing an unrelated task, and when my mind is quiet and singularly focused on an activity.

Before taking on the important task of answering the questions "Who Am I?" "Where Am I?" and "Why Am I?" I spent time in nature and time alone, tapping into my intuition to help center myself and really be able to hear what my inner guidance system wanted me to know. After much soul searching, I was able to provide answers to these three pivotal questions.

Who Am I?

This question defines **who I want to be this in world and what I want to be possible through me by my Beingness.** I chose the following:

- I AM Love in Action
- I AM of Service to Humanity
- I AM a Powerful Educator
- I AM Power and Unlimited Potential
- I AM Unity in Action
- I AM the Creator of My Reality
- I AM a Divine Spiritual Being Who is Fully Connected to Source

Where Am I?

The follow-up questions here are **"Where is my consciousness?"** or **"What are the physics of this reality?"** I chose the following:

- Am I on a planet or in a simulation or a game? I am not sure. I do, however, understand the physics of my world and how my consciousness works within it.
- Our world reflects our thoughts, emotions, and actions. Our world reflects our internal state of Being.
- Our world vibrates in bands of frequency. The higher our frequency, the more expanded our consciousness, and the greater the impact we can have on our reality
- We manifest our reality with our conscious and subconscious minds. We need to be a powerful steward to both minds.
- We are in a world where we have a profound relationship to Ourselves, Others, and Our Environment. Understanding these relationships is key to creating a successful and cherished life.

Why Am I?

This question is about **what I plan to do with my Beingness**. I chose the following:

- To assist humanity through their human awakening journey
- To educate humanity by providing powerful resources that will empower and inspire them
- To help humanity remember their empowering skills and abilities
- To remind humanity of their profound relationship to themselves, other people, and their environment
- To help unite awakened human beings
- To be Love in every moment

- To create a reality for myself and for humanity that is filled with love, power, and possibility
- To help humanity remember our divine spiritual nature while living the human experience

Creating My New Life Plan

One of the key benefits of answering these important questions is that it is a conscious, proactive, and co-creative endeavor. **This activity tells the universe that you are 1) awake and 2) serious about who you intend to Be in this world, and what you plan to do with your new life.** It declares your Beingness, and leaves you with actionable objectives and goals. It is the first step towards consciously creating a new plan of life for yourself and for your future.

Another benefit of this endeavor is that it focuses you, and helps you prioritize what is important to you. **Ultimately, it creates your new reality because what you decide and what you declare becomes your new truth – a new truth that, in turn, co-creates your new world.** It's very powerful! Remember that you create all of this with your thoughts, emotions, and actions!

Once I was able to work through this process and consciously make my decisions, my new path came into focus. I was ready to start a new plan, and I knew that plan would be taking the path that would empower me to help others during their awakening. My new role and my new plan would involve helping other people find, embody, and learn to use the rules and tools that I had found through my research.

One of the best parts of my new plan was that I still had much learning to do myself. I had only scratched the surface of what there truly is to know about being human. I had only acquired some of the information and tools to ignite the divine power within all of us. I was ready to begin and excited to see what else there was to learn, so that I could share my insights with my fellow humans. I was excited to shine my light on the path that awakening humans could take to educate themselves on how this reality works, and to provide them with tools that will empower them. I was ready to help other humans create a life that they loved – one built consciously and one that allows them access to all that is possible! Let's do this!

Chapter 7 Questions

1. Did walking you through my journey and approach to answering the questions posed in Stage 4 – The Choice Stage – give you any insight into how you might approach these questions yourself?
2. Is there anything mentioned in this chapter that you might use as you start to forge your own new path and create your new way of Being and plan of life?

Chapter 8
From Concept to Manifested Reality

"Let a man radically alter his thoughts and he will be
astonished at the rapid transformation
it will effect in the material conditions of his life."
–James Allen

Once I made a conscious decision about my life based on who I want to Be in this world, I was ready to take action to bring my vision from a concept into manifested reality. I was ready to create a new plan for my life, and to manifest it physically.

In order to manifest anything in our reality, it is important to remember our multidimensional nature and our co-creative abilities. It is also important to remember that we live in both the physical or three-dimensional world, and also in a nonphysical or multidimensional world. One key ingredient of manifesting is to be sure that you are taking action in both your physical as well as your non-physical world. The following section outlines the specific action that I took in both worlds to help birth my vision into manifested reality.

Taking Action in Your Physical (Three-Dimensional) World

One way to work within your physical world to manifest a concept into reality is to adopt the perspective of a project manager. As Steven Covey states in his book *The Seven Habits of Highly Effective People*, you must "Begin with the end in mind." (Covey 95)

Once you have a clearly defined end goal, it is prudent to break it down into clearly defined objectives and goals. Then, break down your goals into actionable and tangible steps that will help ensure success. These steps should be measurable so that you can hold yourself accountable and be able to track your progress.

For me to manifest my newly defined purpose of helping my fellow humans through the awakening process, I first had to take action in my physical world. I had to define what it was that I was trying to ultimately accomplish. I had to develop my end-state goal and define specific objectives that would allow me to successfully achieve my vision.

When meditating on my end state, I realized that there were three basic goals that I wanted to accomplish with my new plan:

The first goal was to help people understand and begin to use the power of their mind.

The second goal involved uniting other awakening humans.

The third goal was to create what I define as "Key Foundational Concepts for Being Human" that could take some of the rules and tools I had learned and share them with fellow humans in a way that is tangible, relatable, and easily recognizable.

End State Goal #1: Unlock Your Mind – Unleash Your Power

One basic problem facing humanity is our beautiful minds. There are two basic issues regarding the use of our minds that plague humanity and unknowingly limit our potential. The first is that we identify our brains as our dominant tool when making decisions in our lives. For a long time, humanity has overidentified with intellect and has stopped trusting their intuitive guidance systems, or their guts. Humanity has also stopped listening to their hearts and following what they are guiding them to do.

The second limitation is that we do not understand how our conscious and subconscious minds work. We do not know that we co-create reality, and we do not understand how the role of perception contributes to what we manifest. This is something that we need to understand so that we can begin to manifest what we want – not what we don't want – into our reality. Education on the power of our mind and its role in manifesting reality is crucial.

One of my key objectives became to educate humanity on the role of intuition, and how to use the power of the mind to proactively and consciously create a life they love. I knew that one of the major objectives of my new plan would be to help people unlock their minds and unleash their power.

End State Goal #2: Unite the Awakened – Find the Other Purples

Another key objective of my plan is to unite the awakened. One of the most difficult aspects of the awakening journey is that it is happening to humans at different rates, which leaves many of us feeling isolated and alone. Uniting the awakened is an important part of my new plan for two reasons:

Uniting humanity will help give them a community and a tribe so they do not have to go through the process alone. It will provide a much-needed support system for those who are waking up.

Knowing what I know about the power of our minds, and our individual as well as collective co-creative abilities, uniting awakened humans is the most effective and efficient way to collectively manifest a new world – a world that is filled with love, beauty and compassion. It is the best way for us to create what we want to see in our beautiful world!

When I started to wake up and realized that there would be great power in uniting other awakened souls, I remembered something I had heard years ago from a man named Lee Carroll. Lee Carroll is an American channel, speaker, and author who channels an entity he calls Kryon (Carroll, 2023). In one of Mr. Carroll's channelings, he described a scenario where higher spiritual beings came to Earth to see if it was time for them to intervene. What resonated with me was that these beings were accessing the spiritual evolution of humanity, and that assessment was based on whether "The Purples had found each other" (Carroll 2023). In this scenario, the purples were the human beings that accumulated light, and who held a significant amount of light in their bodies. Relating that to our situation, the purples would be the human beings who have awakened. I'm not sure why I remember this message, but when I awoke and found myself in the situation that I am in right now, **one of my very first instincts was to "find the other purples."**

End State Goal #3: Key Foundational Concepts for Being Human

When looking at the rules and tools outlined in Key Theme #2 found in Chapter 5, I realized these concepts could be categorized differently to be more impactfully embodied by human beings who become familiar with them. I had to help make these concepts tangible, relatable, recognizable, and even actionable. I started thinking about what it would have been like if I had been taught these concepts from birth. Think about it. What would the world be like if these concepts were taught to all humans being born, and reinforced by our parents and other worldly institutions that help mold our perception of reality?

Eventually I asked myself a slightly different, but equally important question:

If someone I loved was coming to Earth for the first time, what would they need to know in order to thrive?

They would have to have a profound understanding of three basic relationships: Relationship to Self, Relationship to Others, and Relationship to the Environment.

Once embodied, these concepts will ensure that human beings thrive.

Key Foundational Concepts for Being Human

Relationship to Self

Embody Self Love: Love is the most powerful force in the universe. Love yourself unconditionally, not just as a concept, but as a way of Being. Lovingly accept all aspects of yourself.

Expect Your Wish Manifested: Act and feel that your wishes are already fulfilled and they will be. Align thoughts and feelings to manifest your dreams.

Manage Your Minds: Practice presence and being conscious; manage your subconscious mind so it is programmed only by you. Envision maximum health at all times!

Raise Your Frequency: Be mindful of your energy and frequency to stay connected to Source and manage your overall well-being. Personify joy! Live in a constant state of gratitude for all that is.

Remember Your Multidimensionality: Remember that you are more than a three-dimensional personality – you are a divine, immortal, and powerful multidimensional being. Celebrate your divine nature! Remember that God lives within you.

OTHERS

Relationship to Others

Be Compassionate: Be compassionate toward your fellow human beings.

Have Empathy: Empathize with other human beings. Put yourself in their shoes.

Respect All Life: Treat all life forms with gentleness and care.

Exemplify Oneness: Be one with everybody and everything. Be in cooperation, not competition, with other human beings.

Radiate Kindness: Be kind to everyone you interact with.

ENVIRONMENT

Relationship to the Environment

Love is King: Love is the most powerful force in the universe and is dominant over all other frequencies

Stay Connected to a Higher Power: Stay connected to a higher power that governs our universe.

Harness the Power of Your Imagination: Use the power of your imagination to tap into your powerful human potential and to create the life you want. Remember that you create your reality with your consciousness and with the power of your intention.

Partner with Mother Earth: Mother Earth is our partner. Treat her with love, gratitude, and respect.

Stand in Your Sovereignty: Sovereignty and freedom are your birthrights. You are not given either by anyone. They are inalienable rights and you should protect both.

Taking Action in Your Non-Physical (Multidimensional) World

The second key component of manifesting is to take action within your multidimensional space by using the power of your mind and all that you have learned about co-creation. While taking action in your physical world is important, it is only half of the equation. Most of the manifesting that occurs in our world happens in higher dimensions of reality, as a result of what we think and how we feel. We co-create our world with the power of our mind and the frequency of our emotions. Given this, I typically use the following techniques when I want to use the power of my consciousness to manifest something into our physical reality. These techniques are what I have been applying to take my vision and new plan from concept to manifested reality.

Active Meditation – Act as If It Already Is!

One of the most powerful concepts that I have uncovered over the past few years is the power of our minds to create this reality and to manifest what we want. There are multiple techniques, but essentially all methods use the power of meditating on a desired outcome as if it has already occurred, with as much detail and positive emotion as possible. An example of this would be trying to manifest a new car. If you were trying to manifest the car of your dreams, you would meditate and visualize the car as if you already owned it. You could picture yourself signing the paperwork and taking ownership of the car keys – a car that you now own. You could then picture how the car smells as you drive it, and how you it feels as the wind blows your hair when you are driving fast. You can picture where you go in your new car and who is with you. You can picture your friends congratulating you on your new purchase, and even picture celebrating five years of ownership.

The point here is to play the scenario out in your mind as if it has already happened. Details are important, and mental imagery is key. Another crucial part of this technique is to feel the emotions as if you already owned the car. The more positive the feelings are – joy, love, gratitude – the better. It is important to remember that your consciousness is what is manifesting our reality, and your subconscious mind – the part where meditation and visualization happen – doesn't know the different between what is real and what is not real. **Make a movie in your mind, picturing and feeling what you want as if it has already happened – then it will!**

Don't Take Your Eye Off the Ball

This popular baseball analogy is appropriate when working within your non-physical space to manifest something that you want. Like keeping your eye on the ball when you're at bat, it is important to keep your desired vision in clear focus. There are numerous distractions in today's external world that can make you lose focus. It is critical that you stay present to your end-state goals and keep them in the forefront of your mind. You can do this by setting time to meditate or performing daily affirmations as a reminder. Whatever your technique, it is important to stay present and remain consciously and consistently vigilant about where you are going and what you are trying to accomplish.

Finding Your Own Game

Part II of this book took you on a journey through the thought process that I used to define my new purpose and my new game plan. It also gave you specific insights into the action I took in both my physical and non-physical worlds to begin to bring my vision into manifested reality. I hope walking you through my journey served as an example and gave you ideas to use when you are trying to do the same.

If you are awake, you are awake for a reason. You have a specific role to play in your personal awakening journey, and a role to contribute to humanity's rise in consciousness. It is time for you to create your own plan.

Part III of this book is your call to action. It is time for you to take the powerful action to start building a new life and a new plan for yourself. The time is now! Chapter 9 invites you

to remember who you are and to take the powerful call to action to create your own new plan. You've got this!

Chapter 8 Questions
1. Are there other techniques, beyond what was mentioned in this chapter, that you can use to take action in your physical world to manifest your vision into reality?
2. What will be your technique in non-physical space to manifest your vision into reality?
3. What are some of your ideas for creating a new plan of life for yourself?

Part III

Chapter 9

Create Your New Game: Join Me!
"Decisions, not conditions, determine what a man is."
—Viktor Frankl

Congratulations! You have made it through one of the most transformational human rites of passage – you are awake! At least, you have started the process of waking up that can very well last a lifetime. Part II of this book took you through my personal journey of awakening and outlined the specifics of how I created a new purpose for myself, and my thought process when creating a new plan for my life. It is time for you to do the same!

It is quite possible that you are still trying to find your footing in your new world. In fact, you may still be somewhat in a reality no man's land, trying to figure out how to integrate your old world with your new world. You may very well still be trying to determine what to do next, and what tangible and actionable steps you need to take to start building and co-creating a new life that you love. This chapter is written to help you do just that.

The following sections detail important concepts that I have researched. I find them to be the most impactful in creating something new and bringing a vision into manifested reality. These concepts are provided to give you tools that you can use as you begin to proactively start to build a new awakened life that is filled with infinite possibility.

Consciously Decide Who You are, Where You Are, and Why You Are

Undoubtedly, the most impactful thing you can do when you are trying to create a new life for yourself and merge your old and new worlds is to begin to construct the answers to the powerful questions posed in Stage 4 of the awakening process detailed in Chapter 6.

Once you wake up, you are not the same person. You have changed, and all previous definitions of yourself and your reasons for Being – your purpose – need to be rewritten. You have learned much about the world you grew up in, and many of your belief systems have shattered. It is time to rebuild. You are ready to redefine a new purpose and reason for Being so that you can get out of your reality no man's land and merge your old and new worlds. You are ready to create your new life. Where do you start?

The best way to start to rebuild your life is to consciously redefine yourself and your purpose by powerfully choosing the answers to the questions "Who am I?" "Where am I?" and "Why am I?" Defining yourself through this lens puts you in a proactive position and alters your experience of life from one where you are reacting to external events in the world to one where you are the co-creator and driver of your experience. **This profound shift in the experience of your relationship to life – proactive not reactive – is the key to moving forward. It will take you out of the rabbit hole and move you beyond what could be years of looking for answers that you may never acquire. It will put you in the drivers seat of your life, where you quickly learn that life is not happening to you. Instead, you are the decision maker and driver of your destiny.** We are here to remember who we are and the power we hold. We are here to build a life that we love and that is filled with every possibility available. Let's go!

Create A New Plan or Many!

Once you have answered the three foundational questions "Who am I?" "Where am I?" and "Why am I?", it is time to create a new plan for your life. Creating a life plan has been discussed in several places throughout the book, but the concept itself has not yet been specifically defined. I define a life plan as a strategy that is created, consciously or unconsciously, to achieve a desired goal based on your notion of what a successful life entails.

Before waking up, the majority of the plans you made were based on mostly unconscious decisions, and ones that in many ways involved strategies to survive your life. In contrast, when you wake up and understand your co-creative abilities, that narrative switches, and you realize that you have the tools to build any life that you want and play any game that you desire. You comprehend that your opportunities and possibilities are limitless.

In Chapter 8, I defined a life plan based on who I have defined myself to Be and how I want to express my Beingness in the world. In that chapter, I detailed my plan and my desired end state. What I did not mention, however, is that this plan, while currently my primary focus, is not the only plan that I have created for my life, and not the only one that I am enacting.

Creating a plan is just a tool that can be used to help you prioritize what is important to you and take the required action to create something new in your life. It is a powerful way to ensure that your defined Beingness becomes a manifested expression in your world. You can make a big plan, such as a plan created around your life's purpose or mission. Likewise, you can also create a smaller plan that is played out on a lesser scale. As an example, you could create a plan based on your defined Being of a healer, and express that Beingness as the owner of a healing center. In parallel, you could make a smaller, but equally important, plan where you simply define your Beingness as that of the best mom in the world. Some plans manifest on a bigger scale than others, but all plans of Beingness are of equal importance.

It does not really matter what plan you make or how many you decide to make. The key is to be sure that you are making a consciously created plan that is proactively aligned with who and why you have defined your Beingness to be. That is what ultimately matters!

Take Action in Your Physical (Three-Dimensional) World

Once a plan is created, it is important that you take action in your physical world to ensure that you can manifest your vision into physicality. As described in Chapter 8, a key aspect of working within your physical world to manifest is to set actionable and measurable steps toward your end-state goals. Sometimes trying something new can feel overwhelming, but breaking your goals down into smaller steps can make it feel less scary and can help hold you accountable for accomplishing what you set out to do. Equally, having measurable steps will enable you to physically see the progress that you are making toward your goals, which will help keep you motivated.

There are numerous management books available and a variety of ways to achieve a three-dimensional goal. Find what works for you and keep going. Just remember that whatever that you have decided to do is important. Pick a management strategy that works for you and just get going!

Take Action in Your Non-Physical (Multidimensional) World

In conjunction with taking action in your physical world to birth your vision into manifested reality, you must also take action in your non-physical world. The key to success in manifesting is to remember that nothing happens in our physical world without first being created in our non-physical reality. **We co-create everything in our physical world by first creating it in our non-physical world. Remember, our external world is a reflection of our internal world. "As Above so Below. As within, So without."** (Trismegistus)

There are multiple books and techniques available that teach you how to use the power of your mind to create your reality. Whether you decide to use meditation, visualization, or affirmations is up to you. What is important, however, is that manifesting anything into physicality requires action in both your physical and in your non-physical world. From a non-physical perspective, thought, emotion, and action are paramount to co-creation.

Remember that You are a Human Being and Not a Human Doing

Transitioning from the perspective of being a human who is doing to one where you are consciously Being is a complete shift in power and to your relationship to your world. The notion of a human doing is analogous to that of a salmon swimming upstream. The salmon might be swimming its hardest, but ultimately it is going against the current and will most likely not achieve its desired goal. In contrast, when I think of a human being, I think of water that simply just flows. Water does not push rocks out of the way; instead, it gently maneuvers around them and continues on its way. Similarly, a human Being is like that water. A human Being is not trying to get somewhere. Instead, a human Being is just Being, and is making a difference simply by who he or she has chosen to Be.

Once you decide who it is you want to Be in this world, you too will make a difference. It does not matter what you choose. All that really matters is that you choose what resonates with your soul. **You are powerful, and your Beingness will ripple out in ways that you may never know and impact people in ways that you can't yet imagine. The key is to remember to show up in this world from a powerful position. That position is gentle – like the water – and happens when you simply follow your heart and express your beautiful Beingness. All the power lies in Being, not in doing.**

Follow Your Heart

In our society, we have been taught to use our intellect and our mental energy to solve problems and to determine our path forward. In your awakened state you will discover that the part of your body that knows what is best for you is not your brain, but your beautiful heart. Some people believe that our heart is actually a portal to higher dimensions, and it is the part of your body that will always know and discern truth. Learn to tap into this powerful resource when you are working through the process of making decisions to create your new life and make a new life plan. Your heart will always steer you in the right direction.

Trust Your Gut

The concept of trusting your gut is a lovely metaphor for tapping into Source and listening to what the universe is trying tell you. The universe is always talking to you and steering you in a direction that is for your highest good. The universe will move you in the direction that is best for you if you afford yourself the opportunity to listen to it. Once you tap into your gut feeling, remember to trust it. Don't defer to your analytical mind to validate your gut feelings. Your gut, in conjunction with your heart, will always steer you to what is in your best interest, and that is typically aligned with the highest good of all. Always trust your gut!

Quiet Your Mind

One of the most important things that you can do when trying to make the decisions that will determine your new plan and your new future is to quiet your mind. It is very difficult in our current day to be still and just be quiet unless you consciously make the time to do just that.

I travel frequently and sometimes observe other people when I am waiting to board my plane. If you ever just take a step back and look at people in the airport, 99 percent of them are looking at their phones. Also, once we board the plane, even if the flight is only an hour, people often frantically hook into their phones so they can begin watching a movie or a television show. Many people are so addicted to the external chatter associated with social media and other entertainment platforms that it doesn't even occur to them to sit quietly and go within.

When creating a new life for yourself, it is imperative that you quiet your mind so that you can tap into the higher dimensions of reality and connect to Source. You will never be able to fully understand what you are being guided to do until you quiet your mind. I believe quieting your mind, whether through meditation or being in nature, is a key element of happiness. It is my personal belief that one of the main reasons that people are depressed and anxious is they don't make the conscious effort to quiet their mind and tap into Source or the multidimensional aspects of themselves. This beautiful multidimensional part of yourself is what will help you stay centered and direct you towards all the information required to live a happy and purposeful life.

Have Compassion but Stand in Your Power

When you go through the awakening process, you change. The world around you, especially family and friends, however, often does not change with you. This can be tricky to navigate if you do not have the tools to assist you with this transition. By now you realize that people are waking up at their own pace, and that you might be somewhat on an island since you have already started on your awakening journey. What you have to keep in mind is that your friends and family, while they still love and want to support you, may not understand what happened to you.

Often people who wake up change many aspects of their lives, such as a job or a relationship, because their new way of being doesn't resonate with what they were doing or with some of the relationships they had before they woke up. Similarly, activities and interests for people who are waking up also change. Many people change their habits, such as what they eat or drink, or even the clothes that they wear. No matter the change, your closest allies will notice.

If this happens to you, there are two basic things that are important to keep in mind:

1) Have compassion for your friends and family. They do not understand why you are no longer being the person you were and why you have changed. This can be scary and difficult for people who love you and who have grown accustomed to you being the person you once were. Compassion is needed here. As you change, often your relationships shift as well. In this case, it is possible to find a middle ground for the relationships that mean most to you. Remember that those who are supposed to stay in your life, will. You may just need to find balance and make a few adjustments, but you can find your footing and make those relationships work.

2) As you start to evolve and begin to branch out and make a bigger plan in life, your friends and family may not understand. Don't forget that they may still be confined by limitations and restrictions of what they believe to be possible that you are no longer bound by. This may be difficult as their doubts may have an effect on you, but you have to push through this. If you have to keep some of your plans a bit quiet until they manifest, then do so. Just remember to stand in your power and stand your ground, in a loving way. Remember to always keep your eye on the ball so that you will continue to successfully manifest your desires into reality.

As always, it is important to stay humble. By no means does the fact that you have woken up make you better than anyone else. If you are awake, then you already know this, but it is worth mentioning. I truly believe that **all** of us – not a selected few – are here to wake up. We are all just at different phases, but still working our way through this beautiful new human rite of passage.

Remember Your Multidimensionality

It is very important to think beyond the three-dimensional nature of who you are and remember that you are a divine being. You are a spirit in a body having a human experience, but you are also a multidimensional piece of our divine creator.

There is so much more to you than what you have been told. If you are here, you are here on purpose. You have a divine mission and reason for Being. It is important to keep this in mind as you start to grow into your new Beingness and into your new life. Remember that you are much more powerful than you can imagine!

Find Your Tribe

It is crucial that you find and connect with other people who are on the awakening journey. Finding your tribe and connecting to a community of like-minded people will provide the support you need as you move forward in your new life. Your tribe and community will be the support system that not only keeps you sane, but also provides much-needed support as you start venturing out and making new plans in your life. The awakening journey can be a lonely experience at times, and a community of people who understands you and what you are going through is worth its weight in gold.

Set an Intention and Ask for Assistance

Another critical tool when creating something new is to set an intention. It is always good to be clear on what you intend to do, and to make that intention known. Setting an intention not only helps to ensure your own clarity of your vision, it also informs the universe of what you are planning to do so that it can begin to align around you and support your vision.

One other important aspect to remember is that you have a lot of help from your non-physical world. I like to think of my non-physical help as My Team. I often call on my team for assistance and guidance. Don't forget that your team and Source want you to succeed. They want you to win this game of life. They are always there waiting for you to simply ask. You have so much support and love on the other side. Always remember to use it. You do this by simply asking, and then being abundantly grateful for all that you receive.

Chapter 9 Questions
1. Which tools mentioned in this chapter resonate with you and inspire you the most, and why?
2. Are any of the tools mentioned in this chapter new concepts for you? If so, which ones? Do you plan to incorporate them into your life as you move forward towards creating a new life and a new plan?
3. What actions do you plan to take now? How many plans will you make?

Chapter 10
Final Thoughts on the Human Awakening Journey
"Go confidently in the direction of your dreams! Live the life you've imagined – "
—Henry David Thoreau

First of all, I want to thank you for reading this book. I sincerely hope that you found some value in it, and are able to walk away with some tools and ideas of where to go next if you are in the process of waking up. I strongly believe that there is a mass spiritual awakening happening on our planet, and that people will need some guidance and direction on how to traverse this new territory when it happens to them. My goal and intention are to help my fellow awakening humans successfully navigate their awakening and effectively make their way through this important new human rite of passage.

Before closing out this book, I would like to leave you with a few final thoughts about waking up and present you with a powerful call to action! You are important, and your contribution to the collective – no matter how big or small – matters. I wish you all the best as you work your way through this amazing journey. All my love to you.

You Hold a Critical Piece of Our Collective Puzzle!

Awakened soul, it is critical that you acknowledge and embody the significance of the role that you play in our collective human awakening story. All awakened souls have an important job and are a key part of this collective awakening process. What you do now truly matters!

If you are awake, then it is critical for you to tap into your intuitive guidance system and take action on what you are being called to do. Now is the time to act. There is no contribution that is too small. **If you are being guided to do something, then it is imperative that you heed that guidance. Whether you know it or not, your contribution – your calling – is a missing piece of our collective puzzle. We need you**!

Find the Other Purples

What is a "Purple?" Purples are truth seekers, way showers, critical thinkers, compassionate, heart centered, strong, and spiritually awake. Purples see through the illusion and false narratives associated with our reality. They are on an unstoppable quest for truth. They understand and have embraced their divine nature, and they know that they have a specific and vital mission to fulfill.

If you **know** that you are a Purple (you feel it in your core), then it is time to fully embrace who you are **and** it is time to find the others. I truly believe that our beautiful human awakening process will quicken once we come together and unite. I know I am a Purple. The question is, are you? If you are reading this, the answer is **absolutely** – You Are! It is time to find the others!

The Awakening Journey is a Continuous and Multilayered Process

Although this book outlines four distinct stages of the human awakening journey, I believe that there may be more that I have yet to experience myself. I am still in the process of evolving and may discover yet another stage of the process as I continue to grow. I reserve the right to reevaluate the stages as I continue to grow and continue my awakening journey.

Additionally, I believe that as people continue to evolve, they will revisit the four stages mentioned in this book, and may even go through each stage a few times. For example, as people grow and learn more, they may want to dive even deeper down the rabbit hole looking for additional answers based on newly acquired insights. Similarly, people may develop more questions and conduct additional data synthesis and analysis activities to make sense of new insights and knowledge. Also, as people expand their consciousness and are able to access more multidimensional information, they may revisit the questions posed in Stage 4 so that they can refine their answers to better align and match who they have become as a result of their continued growth.

The key idea here is that the human awakening journey is about growth and expansion. While you may be able to identify the start of your awakening journey, I do not think that there will be a way to identify a specific end. Once you start evolving, your growth does not stop. I think this is inspiring. Isn't that why we are here, anyways?

Being Human, LLC

As a result of my awakening journey, my husband John and I founded a small company to help me manifest my vision and new Beingness into physicality. To learn more about what we are doing now, you can find us at www.beinghumaninc.com. Peace and massive love to you all!

Endnotes

Chapter 1
"Wake Up." Merriam-Webster Dictionary, Merriam-Webster. http://www.merriam-webster.com. Accessed August 3, 2024.

Wetiko in a Nutshell, Paul Levy. https://innertraditions.com/blog/wetiko-in-a-nutshell. Accessed August 3, 2024.

The Meaning of Maya: The Illusion of the World, Vamadeva Shastri. (January, 15, 2018) https://www.vedanet.com/the-meaning-of-maya-the-illusion-of-the-world. Accessed August 3, 2024.

Chapter 2
"Rite of Passage." Merriam-Webster Dictionary, Merriam-Webster. http://www.merriam-webster.com. Accessed August 3, 2024.

Chapter 3
Shakespeare, William. As You Like It. Edited by Juliet Dusinberre, 3rd edition. The Arden Shakespeare. 2006.

Eckhart on the Dark Night of the Soul, Eckhart Tolle. (July 4, 2024) https://Eckharttolle.com/eckhart-on-the-dark-night-of-the-soul.

"Conspiracy Theory." Merriam-Webster Dictionary, Merriam-Webster. http://www.merriam-webster.com. Accessed August 3, 2024.

Chapter 5
King James Version. https://www.kingjamesbibleonline.org/. Accessed August 5, 2024.

Chapter 8
Covey, Steven R. *The 7 Habits of Highly Effective People*. Simon and Schuster. 1989.

Carroll, Lee. "Kryon: You are Dearly Loved." Kryon. https://www.kryon. com. Accessed September 7, 2023

Chapter 9
Trismegistus, Hermes. *Emerald Table of Hermes*. Between 200 and 800 CE.

Made in the USA
Columbia, SC
28 April 2025